I dedicate this book to the Lord God, Jesus Christ and the Holy Spirit who leads, guides me into all truth.

And

My wonderful, amazing husband Daniel that has always supported me in my dreams and desires to serve God even though it has taken me away from home more days then I ever thought it would. We know that there is no better place to be then in the center of God's will. What joy comes from knowing Him as our personal Lord and Savior.

The Lord prompted me to put this together after spending a weekend at my friend Tracey's house. I was looking for something to get her children. Jaden, Elie, and Landon. That they would know who God says we are in His word.

I am born again which makes me God's Child.

1 Peter 1:23 NIV

²³ For you have been born again, not of perishable seed, but of imperishable, through the living and enduring word of God.

I have Jesus atoning sacrifice 1 John 2:1-2 NIV

2 My dear children, I write this to you so that you will not sin. But if anybody does sin, we have an advocate with the Father—Jesus Christ, the Righteous One. ² He is the atoning sacrifice for our sins, and not only for ours but also for the sins of the whole world.

I am purified, cleansed from sin. 1 John 1:7-9 NIV

⁷ But if we walk in the light, as he is in the light, we have fellowship with one another, and the blood of Jesus, his Son, purifies us from all[a] sin.

⁸ If we claim to be without sin, we deceive ourselves and the truth is not in us. ⁹ If we confess our sins, he is faithful and just and will forgive us our sins and purify us from all unrighteousness.

I am born again into a ne life John 3:16, 1 Peter 1:3 NIV

16 For God so loved the world that he gave his one and only Son, that whoever believes in him shall not perish but have eternal life.

> 1 Peter 1:3 **3** Praise be to the God and Father of our Lord Jesus Christ! In his great mercy he has given us new birth into a living hope through the resurrection of Jesus Christ from the dead,

I am born of God 1 John 5:1 NIV

5 Everyone who believes that Jesus is the Christ is born of God, and everyone who loves the father loves his child as well.

I have eternal life. John 5 :24   6:44   6:47 NIV

5:24 "Very truly I tell you, whoever hears my word and believes him who sent me has eternal life and will not be judged but has crossed over from death to life.

6:44 "No one can come to me unless the Father who sent me draws them, and I will raise them up at the last day. **6:47** Very truly I tell you, the one who believes has eternal life.

I am accepted in Christ. Ephesians 1:6 NIV

6 to the praise of his glorious grace, which he has freely given us in the One he loves.

I am set free. John 8:31 NIV

31 To the Jews who had believed him, Jesus said, "If you   hold to my teaching, you are really my disciples.

I received God's character God is Love. NIV

1 John 4: 16 And so we know and rely on the love God has for us. God is love. Whoever lives in love lives in God, and God in them.

Loves casts out fear. 1 John 4:18 NIV

18 There is no fear in love. But perfect love drives out fear, because fear has to do with punishment. The one who fears is not made perfect in love.

God is light 1 John 1:5 NIV

5 This is the message we have heard from him and declare to you: God is light; in him there is no darkness at all.

A sound mind 2 Timothy 1:7 NIV

7 For the Spirit God gave us does not make us timid, but gives us power, love and self-discipline.

Love 1 Corinthian 13:4-8 NIV

4 Love is patient, love is kind. It does not envy, it does not boast, it is not proud. 5 It does not dishonor others, it is not self-seeking, it is not easily angered, it keeps no record of wrongs. 6 Love does not delight in evil but rejoices with the truth. 7 It always protects, always trusts, always hopes, always perseveres.

8 Love never fails. But where there are prophecies, they will cease; where there are tongues, they will be stilled; where there is knowledge, it will pass away.

Fruit of the Spirit Galatian 5:22-23 NIV

22 But the fruit of the Spirit is love, joy, peace, forbearance, kindness, goodness, faithfulness, **23** gentleness and self-control. Against such things there is no law.

I am called of God. 2 Timothy 1:9 NIV

9 He has saved us and called us to a holy life—not because of anything we have done but because of his own purpose and grace. This grace was given us in Christ Jesus before the beginning of time,

I am call of God by my name Isaiah 43:1 49:1 NIV

43 But now, this is what the Lord says—
he who created you, Jacob,
he who formed you, Israel:
"Do not fear, for I have redeemed you;
I have summoned you by name; you are mine.

49 Listen to me, you islands;
hear this, you distant nations:
Before I was born the Lord called me;
from my mother's womb he has spoken my name.

I am engraved in the palm of God Isaiah 49:16 NIV

16 See, I have engraved you on the palms of my hands;
your walls are ever before me.

I am precious to God, Honored by Him Isaiah 43:4 NIV

Since you are precious and honored in my sight,
and because I love you,
I will give people in exchange for you,
nations in exchange for your life.

I am created by God in the womb PS 139:13-16 NIV

13 For you created my inmost being;
you knit me together in my mother's womb.
14 I praise you because I am fearfully and wonderfully
made; your works are wonderful,
I know that full well.
15 My frame was not hidden from you
when I was made in the secret place,
when I was woven together in the depths of the
earth. 16 Your eyes saw my unformed body;
all the days ordained for me were written in your
book before one of them came to be.

I am formed and set me by God Jeremiah 1:5 NIV

5 5 "Before I formed you in the womb I knew[a] you,
before you were born I set you apart;
I appointed you as a prophet to the nations."

I am called in God by righteousness Isaiah 42:6 NIV

6 "I, the LORD, have called you in righteousness;
  I will take hold of your hand.
  I will keep you and will make you
  to be a covenant for the people
  and a light for the Gentiles,

I am created for His glory Isaiah 43:7 NIV

7 everyone who is called by my name,
  whom I created for my glory,
  whom I formed and made."

I am forgiven Ephesians 1:7 NIV

7 In him we have redemption through his blood, the forgiveness of sins, in accordance with the riches of God's grace.

I am delivered from darkness Colossians 1:13 NIV

13 For he has rescued us from the dominion of darkness and brought us into the kingdom of the Son he loves,

I am a new creature 2 Corinthian 5:17 NIV

[17] Therefore, if anyone is in Christ, the new creation has come:[a] The old has gone, the new is here!

I have God's unfailing love Psalms 32:10 NIV

[10] Many are the woes of the wicked,
  but the LORD's unfailing love
  surrounds the one who trusts in him.

I am loved 1 John 4:10 4:19 NIV

[10] This is love: not that we loved God, but that he loved us and sent his Son as an atoning sacrifice for our sins.

[19] We love because he first loved us.

I have a purpose for living Jer. 29:11 Eph 1:11-12 NIV

[11] For I know the plans I have for you," declares the LORD, "plans to prosper you and not to harm you, plans to give you hope and a future.

Eph 1: [11] In him we were also chosen,[a] having been predestined according to the plan of him who works out everything in conformity with the purpose of his will, [12] in order that we, who were the first to put our hope in Christ, might be for the praise of his glory.

I am never forsaken Psalms 27:10 MEV

10 If my father and my mother forsake me,
then the LORD will take me in.

I am comforted Isaiah 66:13 TLB

13 I will comfort you there as a little one is comforted by its mother.

I have a Father Psalms 68:5 ICB

You answer us in amazing ways,
God our Savior. People everywhere on the earth
and beyond the sea trust you.

I am not an orphan John 14:18 ICB

18 "I will not leave you all alone like orphans. I will come back to you.

I am adopted by God Ephesians 1:5 ICB

5 And before the world was made, God decided to make us his own children through Jesus Christ. That was what he wanted and what pleased him.

I am filled with the Holy Spirit in unity John 14:16, John 19:20 ICB

16 I will ask the Father, and he will give you another Helper.[a] He will give you this Helper to be with you forever.

20 The sign was written in the Jewish language, in Latin, and in Greek. Many of the Jews read the sign, because this place where Jesus was killed was near the city.

I have the Holy Spirit to teach me. 1John 2:27 ICB

27 Christ gave you a special gift. You still have this gift in you. So you do not need any other teacher. The gift he gave you teaches you about everything. This gift is true, not false. So continue to live in Christ, as his gift taught you.

I am the temple of the Holy Spirit. I Corinthians 6:19 ICB

19 You should know that your body is a temple for the Holy Spirit. The Holy Spirit is in you. You have received the Holy Spirit from God. You do not own yourselves.

I am washed, sanctified and justified. 1 Corinthians 6:11 ICB

11 In the past, some of you were like that. But you were washed clean. You were made holy. And you were made right with God in the name of the Lord Jesus Christ and by the Spirit of our God.:

I am an overcomer Romans 8:9-11 ICB

9 But you are not ruled by your sinful selves. You are ruled by the Spirit, if that Spirit of God really lives in you. But if anyone does not have the Spirit of Christ, then he does not belong to Christ. **10** Your body will always be dead because of sin. But if Christ is in you, then the Spirit gives you life, because Christ made you right with God. **11** God raised Jesus from death. And if God's Spirit is living in you, then he will also give life to your bodies that die. God is the One who raised Christ from death. And he will give life through[a] his Spirit that lives in you.

I am transformed. Romans 12:2 ICB

2 Do not be shaped by this world. Instead be changed within by a new way of thinking. Then you will be able to decide what God wants for you. And you will be able to know what is good and pleasing to God and what is perfect.

I am not afraid Hebrews 13:6 ICB

6 So we can feel sure and say,

"I will not be afraid because the Lord is my helper.
   People can't do anything to me." *Psalm 118:6*

I am redeemed from the curse. Galatians 3:13 ICB

13 So the law put a curse on us, but Christ took away that curse. He changed places with us and put himself under that curse. It is written in the Scriptures, "Everyone whose body is displayed on a tree[a] is cursed."

I am strong in the Lord. Eph 6:10 ICB

10 Finally, be strong in the Lord and in his great power.

I am holy and with out blame before Him. Eph 1:4 ICB

4 In Christ, he chose us before the world was made. In his love he chose us to be his holy people—people without blame before him.

I am blessed. Deuteronomy 28:1-14 ICB

28:1 You must completely obey the Lord your God. And you must carefully follow all his commands I am giving you today. Then the Lord your God will make you greater than any other nation on earth. **2** Obey the Lord your God. Then all these blessings will come and stay with you:

3 You will be blessed in the city. You will be blessed in the country.

4 Your children will be blessed. Your crops will be blessed. Your cattle will be blessed with calves and your sheep with lambs.

5 Your basket and your kitchen will be blessed.

6 You will be blessed when you come in and when you go out.

7 The Lord will let you defeat the enemies that come to fight you. They will attack you from one direction. But they will run from you in seven directions.

8 The Lord your God will bless you with full barns. He will bless everything you do. He will bless the land he is giving you.

9 The Lord will make you his holy people, as he promised. But you must obey his commands. You must do what he wants you to do. 10 Then everyone on earth will see that you are the Lord's people. They will be afraid of you. 11 The Lord will make you rich. You will have many children. Your cattle will have many calves. Your land will give good crops. It is the land that the Lord promised your ancestors he would give to you.

12 The Lord will open up his storehouse. The skies will send rain on your land at the right time. And he will bless everything you do. You will lend to other nations. But you will not need to borrow from them. 13 The Lord will make you like the head and not like the tail. You will be on top and not on bottom. But you must obey the commands of the Lord your God that I am giving you today. Be careful to keep them. 14 Do not disobey anything I command you today. Do exactly as I command. Do not follow other gods or serve them.

I am a saint. Romans 1:7 ICB

7 This letter is to all of you in Rome whom God loves and has called to be his holy people.

May God our Father and the Lord Jesus Christ show you kindness and give you peace.

I am qualified to share His inheritance. Col 1:12 ICB

12 Then you will joyfully give thanks to the Father. He has made you[a] able to have all that he has prepared for his people who live in the light..

I am the head and not the tail. I am above and not beneath. Deuteronomy 28:13 ICB

13 The Lord will make you like the head and not like the tail. You will be on top and not on bottom. But you must obey the commands of the Lord your God that I am giving you today. Be careful to keep them.

I am victorious. Revelation. 21:7 ICB

7 Anyone who wins the victory will receive this. And I will be his God, and he will be my son.

I am dead to sin. Romans 6:2 & 6:11 ICB

2 No! We died to our old sinful lives. So how can we continue living with sin?

11 In the same way, you should see yourselves as being dead to the power of sin and alive with God through Christ Jesus.

I am elect. Colossians 3:12 ICB

12 God has chosen you and made you his holy people. He loves you. So always do these things: Show mercy to others; be kind, humble, gentle, and patient.

I am loved with a everlasting love. Jeremiah 31:3 ICB

[3] And from far away the Lord appeared to his people. He said,
"I love you people with a love that will last forever.
I became your friend because of my love and kindness.

I am established to the end. 1 Corinthians 1:8 ICB

[8] Jesus will keep you strong until the end. He will keep you strong, so that there will be no wrong in you on the day our Lord Jesus Christ comes again.

I am circumcised by Christ. Colossians 2:11 ICB

[11] In Christ you had a different kind of circumcision. That circumcision was not done by hands. I mean, you were made free from the power of your sinful self. That is the kind of circumcision Christ does.

I am crucified with Christ. Galatians 2:20 ICB

[20] I do not live anymore—it is Christ living in me. I still live in my body, but I live by faith in the Son of God. He loved me and gave himself to save me.

I am alive with Christ. Ephesians 2:5 ICB

[5] We were spiritually dead because of the things we did wrong against God. But God gave us new life with Christ. You have been saved by God's grace.

I am raised up in Christ. Ephesians 2:8 TLB

[8] Because of his kindness, you have been saved through trusting Christ. And even trusting is not of yourselves;[a] it too is a gift from God.

I am his faithful follower. Ephesians 5:1 TLB

Follow God's example in everything you do just as a much loved child imitates his father.

I am the light of the world. Matthew 5:14 TLB

You are the world's light—a city on a hill, glowing in the night for all to see.

I am the salt of the earth. Matthew 5:13 TLB

 "You are the world's seasoning, to make it tolerable. If you lose your flavor, what will happen to the world? And you yourselves will be thrown out and trampled underfoot as worthless.

I am called of God. 2 Timothy 1:9 TLB

[9] It is he who saved us and chose us for his holy work not because we deserved it but because that was his plan long before the world began—to show his love and kindness to us through Christ.

I am brought by the blood of Christ. Eph. 2:13 TLB

13 But now you belong to Christ Jesus, and though you once were far away from God, now you have been brought very near to him because of what Jesus Christ has done for you with his blood.

I am more than a conqueror. Romans 8:37 TLB

37 but despite all this, overwhelming victory is ours through Christ who loved us enough to die for us

I am in Christ Jesus by God's doing. 1 Cor. 1:30 TLB

30 For it is from God alone that you have your life through Christ Jesus. He showed us God's plan of salvation; he was the one who made us acceptable to God; he made us pure and holy[a] and gave himself to purchase our salvation.*

I am an ambassador for Christ. 2 Corinthians 5:20 TLB

20 We are Christ's ambassadors. God is using us to speak to you: we beg you, as though Christ himself were here pleading with you, receive the love he offers you—be reconciled to God.

I am beloved and chosen by God. 1 Thessalonians 1:4 NIV

4 For we know, brothers and sisters[a] loved by God, that he has chosen you,

I am the first fruit among his creation. James 1:18 NIV

¹⁸ He chose to give us birth through the word of truth, that we might be a kind of firstfruits of all he created.

I am born of God, satan can't touch me. 1 john 5:18 TLB

¹⁸ No one who has become part of God's family makes a practice of sinning, for Christ, God's Son, holds him securely, and the devil cannot get his hands on him.

I am a king and a priest unto God. Revelation 1:6 TLB

⁶ He has gathered us into his Kingdom and made us priests of God his Father. Give to him everlasting glory! He rules forever! Amen!

I am Chosen. 1 Peter 2:9 TLB

⁹ But you are not like that, for you have been chosen by God himself—you are priests of the King, you are holy and pure, you are God's very own—all this so that you may show to others how God called you out of the darkness into his wonderful light.

I am perfect. Hebrews 10:14 TLB

¹⁴ For by that one offering he made forever perfect in the sight of God all those whom he is making holy.

I am joint heir with Christ. Romans 8:17 TLB

17 And since we are his children, we will share his treasures—for all God gives to his Son Jesus is now ours too. But if we are to share his glory, we must also share his suffering.

I am reconciled to God. 2 Corinthians 5:18 NIV

18 All this is from God, who reconciled us to himself through Christ and gave us the ministry of reconciliation:

I am forgiven and healed. Ps. 103:3 and 12   TLB

3 He forgives all my sins. He heals me.,

12 He has removed our sins as far away from us as the east is from the west.

I am healed by the wounds of Jesus. 1 Peter 2:24 TLB

24 He personally carried the load of our sins in his own body when he died on the cross so that we can be finished with sin and live a good life from now on. For his wounds have healed ours!

I am in the world as He is in heaven. 1 John 4:17 TLB

17 And as we live with Christ, our love grows more perfect and complete; so we will not be ashamed and embarrassed at the day of judgment, but can face him with confidence and joy because he loves us and we love him too.

I am a fellow citizen with the saints Ephesians 2:19 TLB

[19] Now you are no longer strangers to God and foreigners to heaven, but you are members of God's very own family, citizens of God's country, and you belong in God's household with every other Christian.

I am sealed with the Spirit Ephesians 1:13 TLB

[13] And because of what Christ did, all you others too, who heard the Good News about how to be saved, and trusted Christ, were marked as belonging to Christ by the Holy Spirit, who long ago had been promised to all of us Christians.

I am complete in Christ. Colossians 2:10 TLB

[0] *so you have everything when you have Christ,* and you are filled with God through your union with Christ. He is the highest Ruler, with authority over every other power.

I am free from condemnation. Romans 8:1 TLB

So there is now no condemnation awaiting those who belong to Christ Jesus.

I am the righteousness of God. 2 Corinthians 5:21 TLB

For God took the sinless Christ and poured into him our sins. Then, in exchange, he poured God's goodness into us!

I am firmly rooted. Colossians 2:7 TLB

7 Let your roots grow down into him and draw up nourishment from him. See that you go on growing in the Lord, and become strong and vigorous in the truth you were taught. Let your lives overflow with joy and thanksgiving for all he has done.

I have Joy. Galatians 5:22 Philippians 4:4 TLB

22 But when the Holy Spirit controls our lives he will produce this kind of fruit in us: love, joy, peace, patience, kindness, goodness, faithfulness

4 Always be full of joy in the Lord; I say it again, rejoice!

I have peace beyond understanding. Galatians 5:22 Philippians 4:6 TLB

22 But when the Holy Spirit controls our lives he will produce this kind of fruit in us: love, joy, peace, patience, kindness, goodness, faithfulness,

6 Don't worry about anything; instead, pray about everything; tell God your needs, and don't forget to thank him for his answers.

I think a new way. Philippians 4:8-9 TLB

8 And now, brothers, as I close this letter, let me say this one more thing: Fix your thoughts on what is true and good and right. Think about things that are pure and lovely, and dwell on the fine, good things in others. Think about all you can praise God for and be glad about. **9** Keep putting into practice all you learned from me and saw me doing, and the God of peace will be with you..

I am a disciple of Christ. John 13:34-35 NKJV

34 A new commandment I give to you, that you love one another; as I have loved you, that you also love one another. **35** By this all will know that you are My disciples, if you have love for one another."

I am built on the foundation. Ephesians 2:20 NKJV

20 having been built on the foundation of the apostles and prophets, Jesus Christ Himself being the chief cornerstone,

I am a partaker od His divine nature. 2 Peter 1:4 NKJV

4 by which have been given to us exceedingly great and precious promises, that through these you may be partakers of the divine nature, having escaped the [a]corruption *that is* in the world through lust.

I am God's workmanship. Ephesians 2:10 NKJV

. **10** For we are His workmanship, created in Christ Jesus for good works, which God prepared beforehand that we should walk in them.

I am being changed into His image. Philippians 1:6 NKJV

6 being confident of this very thing, that He who has begun a good work in you will complete *it* until the day of Jesus Christ;

Romans 8:29-30 NKJV

29 For whom He foreknew, He also predestined *to be* conformed to the image of His Son, that He might be the firstborn among many brethren. **30** Moreover whom He predestined, these He also called; whom He called, these He also justified; and whom He justified, these He also glorified.

I am one with Christ. John 17:21-23 NKJV

21 that they all may be one, as You, Father, *are* in Me, and I in You; that they also may be one in Us, that the world may believe that You sent Me. **22** And the glory which You gave Me I have given them, that they may be one just as We are one: **23** I in them, and You in Me; that they may be made perfect in one, and that the world may know that You have sent Me, and have loved them as You have loved Me.

I have all my needs met in Christ. Philippians 4:19 NKJV

19 And my God shall supply all your need according to His riches in glory by Christ Jesus.

I have the mind of Christ. 1 Corinthians 2:16 NKJV

16 For "who has known the mind of the LORD that he may instruct Him?" But we have the mind of Christ.

I have eternal life. John 6:47 John 17:3 1 John 5:11 NKJV

6:47 Most assuredly, I say to you, he who believes [a]in Me has everlasting life.

17: **3** And this is eternal life, that they may know You, the only true God, and Jesus Christ whom You have sent.

5: **11** And this is the testimony: that God has given us eternal life, and this life is in His Son.

I have guaranteed inheritance. Ephesians 1:14 NKJV

14 who[a] is the [b]guarantee of our inheritance until the redemption of the purchased possession, to the praise of His glory.

I have abundant life. John 10:10 NKJV

10 The thief does not come except to steal, and to kill, and to destroy. I have come that they may have life, and that they may have *it* more abundantly.

I Have over come the world. 1 John 5:4-5 NKJV

4 For whatever is born of God overcomes the world. And this is the victory that has overcome the world—[a]our faith. **5** Who is he who overcomes the world, but he who believes that Jesus is the Son of God?

I have the power to control my thoughts 2 Corinthian 10:5 NKJV

⁵ casting down arguments and every high thing that exalts itself against the knowledge of God, bringing every thought into captivity to the obedience of Christ,

I have access to the Father. Ephesians 2:18 NKJV

¹⁸ For through Him we both have access by one Spirit to the Father.

I have received the power of the Holy Spirit. Mark 16:17 NKJV

¹⁷ And these signs will follow those who [a]believe: In My name they will cast out demons; they will speak with new tongues;

I can do all things through Christ. Philippians 4:13 NKJV

¹³ I can do all things through [a]Christ who strengthens me.

I shall do greater works than Jesus. John 14:12 NKJV

¹² "Most assuredly, I say to you, he who believes in Me, the works that I do he will do also; and greater *works* than these he will do, because I go to My Father.

I walk in Christ Jesus. Colossians 2:6 KNJV

⁶ As you therefore have received Christ Jesus the Lord, so walk in Him,

I possess the Greater One. 1 John 4:4 NKJV

4 You are of God, little children, and have overcome them, because He who is in you is greater than he who is in the world.

I press towards the goal. Philippians 3:14 NKJV

14 I press toward the goal for the prize of the upward call of God in Christ Jesus.

I forget the past and go forward. Philippians 3:12-13 NKJV

12 Not that I have already attained,[a] or am already perfected; but I press on, that I may lay hold of that for which Christ Jesus has also laid hold of me. 13 Brethren, I do not count myself to have [b]apprehended; but one thing *I do*, forgetting those things which are behind and reaching forward to those things which are ahead,

I have received power. Philippians 3:10 NKJV

10 that I may know Him and the power of His resurrection, and the fellowship of His sufferings, being conformed to His death,

I live by the law of the Holy Spirit. Romans 8:2 NKJV

2 For the law of the Spirit of life in Christ Jesus has made me free from the law of sin and death.

I know God's voice. John 10:14 John 10:16 NKJV

14 I am the good shepherd; and I know My *sheep*, and am known by My own.

16 And other sheep I have which are not of this fold; them also I must bring, and they will hear My voice; and there will be one flock *and* one shepherd.

I show forth his praise. 1 Peter 2:9 NKJV

9 But you *are* a chosen generation, a royal priesthood, a holy nation, His own special people, that you may proclaim the praises of Him who called you out of darkness into His marvelous light;

I always triumph in Christ. 2 Corinthians 2:14 NKJV

14 or to governors, as to those who are sent by him for the punishment of evildoers and *for the* praise of those who do good.

I have the fullness of God in Christ. Colossians 2:9-10 NKJV

9 For in Him dwells all the fullness of the Godhead ᵃbodily; **10** and you are complete in Him, who is the head of all ᵇprincipality and power.

Christ is in me hope of glory. Colossians 1:27 NKJV

27 To them God willed to make known what are the riches of the glory of this mystery among the Gentiles: ᵃwhich is Christ in you, the hope of glory.

I am a witness for Christ. Acts 1:8 NKJV

8 But you shall receive power when the Holy Spirit has come upon you; and you shall be ᴸᵃᴵwitnesses to Me in Jerusalem, and in all Judea and Samaria, and to the end of the earth."

I am unconditionally loved. Romans 5:5 1 John 4:8,10 NKJV

5 Now hope does not disappoint, because the love of God has been poured out in our hearts by the Holy Spirit who was given to us.

8 He who does not love does not know God, for God is love.

10 In this is love, not that we loved God, but that He loved us and sent His Son *to be* the propitiation for our sins.

I am the apple of my father's eye. Psalms 17:8 NKJV

8 Keep me as the ᴸᵃᴵapple of Your eye;
Hide me under the shadow of Your wings,

I am being made Holy. Hebrews 10:10 1 Peter 1:16 NKJV

10 By that will we have been ᴸᵃᴵsanctified through the offering of the body of Jesus Christ once *for all.*

16 because it is written, "Be holy, for I am holy."

I am an image bearer. Genesis 1:27 NKJV

²⁷ So God created man in His *own* image; in the image of God He created him; male and female He created them.

I am to rule in heaven with Christ. Revelation 22:5 NKJV

⁵ There shall be no night there: They need no lamp nor light of the sun, for the Lord God gives them light. And they shall reign forever and ever.

I GIVE THANKS TO THE LORD JESUS CHRIST for putting it on my heart to put this booklet together and allow me to complete it in 3 days.

Made in the USA
Columbia, SC
19 November 2020